LEADING STRATEGIC
COMMUNITY CHANGE:
A Primer for Pastors, Church Boards, and Executive Ministry Teams

Jimmy Arthur Atkins

A publication of

The American Journal of Biblical Theology
Illuminating God's Word

Hayesville, NC 28904

www.biblicaltheology.com

Copyright © 2020, Dr. Jimmy Arthur Atkins

All rights reserved. No part of this book may be reproduced, in any form or by any means, without permission in writing from the publisher.

Printed in the United States of America

ISBN: 978-1674884226 (Paperback)

The Lord works from the inside out. The world works from the outside in. The world would take people out of the slum. Christ takes the slum out of people, and then they take themselves out of the slums. The world would mold men by changing their environment. Christ changes men, who then change their environment. The world would shape human behavior, but Christ can change human nature.

Ezra Taft Benson

Churches are needed to serve the large numbers of people who need meditative help if their alienation is to be healed and wholeness of life achieved, but I regret that for the most part, churches do not seem to be serving well. They can be helped to do much better.

Robert K. Greenleaf, author of Servant leadership: A journey into the nature of legitimate power & greatness.

Table of Contents

Dedications vii

Introduction ix

Chapter 1: Why Churches Should Serve 1

Chapter 2: Understanding the Dynamics of Community 5

Chapter 3: Discovering Core Values 15

Chapter 4: Evaluating Organizational Ministry Capacity 25

Chapter 5: Overview of Strategic Planning 33

Chapter 6: Surveying the Land 47

Chapter 7: Strategic Planning Step by Step 57

Chapter 8: Leadership for Community Change 65

Chapter 9: Concluding Thoughts 71

References 73

About the Author 83

Appendix A: Sample Strategic Planning Exercises 85

Appendix B: Strategic Planning Handouts 89

Appendix C: Grant Writing 97

Dedications

First and foremost, this book is dedicated to God and my Lord and Savior, Jesus Christ. With Christ, my life has been transformed for the better. I am humbled by God's call upon my life and His love and kindness He continues to demonstrate towards me.

This book is also dedicated to everyone who believed in me. I am forever grateful to my parents: my father George E. Atkins Sr., who passed away during my junior year in college, and my mother, Olivia, for their guidance, encouragement, and setting an example of hard work and perseverance.

I also dedicate this book to my wife, Kecia, who has always been a source of love and support. Her encouragement along the way has kept me motivated.

I also dedicate this book to my two sons, James Everett and George Walter. I am excited about their future and what God is going to accomplish in their lives.

I dedicate this book to my brothers and sisters and extended family who continue to encourage and support me. Last, but certainly not least, I also dedicate this book to my True Worship Christian Fellowship family and friends who are the best church in the world.

Introduction

Write down the revelation and make it plain on tablets so that a herald may run with it. For the revelation awaits an appointed time, Habakkuk 2:2-3a, NIV

Leading Strategic Community Change is a culmination of my many years of experience in Christian ministry, higher education, leadership development, and consulting with churches and faith-based organizations. As a pastor and leadership practitioner, my thinking has been shaped by my childhood experience growing up in the small town of Gaston, NC where church served as one of few outlets by which youth could find solace. Moreover, it was the local church—Cool Spring Missionary Baptist Church, that organized to provide material and spiritual support to my family when we lost our home in a fire. Thus, I have long believed that the church it at her best when it is demonstrating care and compassion for people in need.

This book explores the dynamics of leadership and strategic community change for churches and faith-based organizations. In doing so, it incorporates principles and practices from the fields of strategic planning, leadership, and organizational development.

At the end of chapters there are exercises designed to reinforce the concepts discussed in the chapter. The appendices also include activities for churches and faith-based organizations to use with their congregations, boards, and executive ministry teams to develop a more effective plan for engaging the community in social and economic change.

Leading Strategic Community Change is based on the fundamental belief that churches and faith-based organizations are often closest to the needs of the poor and disenfranchised, but often lack the capital, human and financial, to implement community-based initiatives that lead to lasting change. However, if given the knowledge and expertise, churches and faith-based organizations can transform their surrounding communities and restore a sense of hope and renewal.

Leading Strategic Community Change is also focused on providing church and faith-based leaders with a practical approach to strategy formation, planning, and organizational development for social change and community engagement. After reading this book, pastors, ministry leaders, and practitioners will gain knowledge and practical skills that will help them to:

1. Define and understand the principles of community-based development
2. Understand the importance of values as a foundation for community-based development
3. Learn organizational development concepts such as mission, vision, and organizational culture.

4. Expand knowledge of strategy, strategy formation, and strategic planning.
5. Understand leadership competencies for leading change in the community.
6. Improve the practice of strategic planning for churches to achieve their community-based development vision.

CHAPTER 1

Why Churches Should Serve

Then I heard a voice of the Lord saying, Whom shall I send? And who will go for us? And I said, Here I am, Send me, Isaiah 6:8, NIV

Churches and faith-based organizations have several inherent strengths that make them strong allies for community change and development. Specifically, churches are established, have considerable knowledge of their communities, and are committed to serving the spiritual and material needs of others. Religious leaders are also strong advocates for social change because they have a firm grounding in spirituality and humanitarian values (Nygren, 1994). Moreover, churches and faith-based organizations have extensive networks and can mobilize volunteers and raise support and awareness around issues in ways that government and private sector organizations cannot achieve on their own. However, too often local institutions are not seen or engaged as potential partners in the community. Simply put, local leaders, planners, and policy makers do not view partnerships with churches as viable alternatives. We can only wonder what could happen is churches and faith-based organizations were given a seat at the proverbial table when plans for the community are being drawn up. Churches and faith-based organizations should be viewed as communities with social influence, economic power, and a leadership networks that can be leveraged to address problems impacting the community.

Strategic and Organizational Challenges

Although churches and faith-based organizations have inherent strengths, they remain confronted with leadership and organizational development challenges that undermine their ability to achieve strategic results. In a 2004 report by Open Source Leadership Strategies entitled *Funding & faith: Research about faith-based organizations and institutions* it was argued that faith-based institutions need capacity building in the areas of strategic planning, staff development, and collaboration. The report states:

> Amidst these many strengths, along with the immeasurable power of faith itself, it can be easy to over-estimate the capacity of churches and church leaders to work and effect change on longstanding, complex community problems. Pastors must spend their time on pastoral duties. Despite the best intentions, they have little extra time to run a FBO at the same time that they may not have the luxury – or the management skills – to delegate these responsibilities to others (p. 17).

Furthermore, church leaders can be overly zealous about their visions without examining their core organizational capacity to implement the vision. Hoyle (1995) states, "impatient managers who run with a vision too fast for those who must make the vision happen will never see the vision fulfilled" (p.39). Moreover, Hoyle asserts that visions succeed with careful planning, time for reflection, and adequate resource allocation. Without a strategic vision, many church leaders run the risk of doing more harm than good in communities they wish to serve.

Research on social services programs underscore that churches frequently undertake programs that provide short-term benefits (i.e., emergency food or utility assistance) rather than programs with sustained involvement to meet longer goals (Chaves, 2001). Perhaps we are asking too much of our churches given the grave problems facing society.

Churches and faith-based organizations are often run and managed by a dedicated pool of volunteers, which present some challenges. Volunteers may have the heart to serve but may have little training or expertise to tackle complex community change initiatives. However, faith gives access to a higher power who in turn can provide resources to accomplish strategic goals.

I believe the most effective churches and faith-based organizations who are great at leading social change are the ones who have community change in their DNA. Essentially, it is who they are and what they are about. Hence, churches and faith-based organizations should consider the costs of failure and success, the people who will benefit, and outcomes they seek first before launching out into the deep and uncertain waters of community change.

CHAPTER 2

Understanding the Dynamics of Community

All the believers were together and had everything in common. They sold property and possessions to give to anyone who had need.
Acts 2:44-45, NIV

I began my career in housing and community development as an intern for a community action agency in Maryland. The Executive Director at the time was and still is regarded as one of the most innovative and dedicated community development leaders in the country. I was very fortunate to have the opportunity to learn from him.

I worked on a community planning and needs assessment study for an old mining town that had been experiencing economic decline and an exodus of population as employment in the mining industry disappeared. With the help of the community, I designed a survey to ascertain the needs and aspirations of the community.

What we discovered was not at all shocking, but eye- opening in the sense that like so many communities, this small town felt neglected and forgotten. Unfortunately, some churches and aid groups have what is called the messiah complex. They show up with a package of pre-fabricated ideas and solutions without bothering to listen first to the community. They think they are all-knowing and all-powerful and without them, the ills of the community cannot be cured.

My view and understanding of community development is more inclusive and expansive. Community development is first and foremost about people. Without people, there can be no real community. Thus, community development is a people-and principle-centered approach to developing and implementing strategies that address strategic community needs such as poverty and drug addiction. Community development is a means to an end and not an end in itself. The essence of community development lies in the doing and not necessarily in the outcome (Theodori, 2005).

Nonetheless, the notion of community and development has alternative meanings. For instance, community may refer to a geographically defined territory. Vital and Keating (2004) contend that community development is a place-based approach that creates assets for people in poor neighborhoods. For instance, affordable housing is a placed-based approach that is used by governments and not-for-profit organizations to build assets and wealth in poor communities.

Community may also refer to social categories such as Hispanic, African American, or religious community. Within this framework, a community may have diverse worldviews, values, and experiences that make it unique. However, it would be wrong to assume that racial and ethnic groups are monolithic in their thoughts and actions. This can lead to stereotyping, which can have negative influences on the outcomes you seek.

A community may also be described as a dynamic system, an interconnected system of institutions such as banking, education, and healthcare (Tamas, Whitmore, & Almonte 2000). Within this framework, a community is influenced by its environment. When there is a breakdown in one part of the system, it has an impact on another. For example, the economic downturn has impacted communities through the loss of jobs, credit, housing, etc. Membership and volunteerism at church have been impacted because families and individuals have been forced to move due to a loss of employment or their homes. The image of a community as a dynamic system stresses the interconnectedness of people and institutions. When this system is working properly, it generates feelings of pride and stability.

John Gardner, former U.S Secretary of Health, Education, and Welfare argues in his book, *On Leadership* that creating a sense of community today is challenging because of the heterogeneity of the population with which one deals. Indeed, we live in a diverse and pluralistic society, one where many beliefs and traditions coexist. Gardner argues that communities must be more than geographic locations. He suggests that the fundamental ingredients of community include: sense of wholeness, shared values, community, caring, trust, and participation and sharing of leadership tasks. In my view, the sharing of leadership tasks is very important because it is more inclusive and builds the capacity of the community to do for itself. Essentially, the community has to assume ownership and responsibility of the process if results are to be sustainable.

On the other hand, the term development often conjures up images of the physical and built environment. Developers build housing, commercial buildings, shopping centers, etc. These developments provide tangible evidence of community change—whether good or bad. This type of development typically receives more attention from government, advocacy groups, and philanthropic organizations. The construction of 50 units of affordable housing in a distressed community is an outcome that is hard to ignore. This intense focus on improving the physical characteristics of a community sometimes overlooks social elements and the people who also make up the community.

There is a need to develop a more comprehensive approach that includes the social dynamics of community development (Chaskin, Joseph, & Chipenda-Dansokho, 1997). For example, when I worked for a large state housing and community development organization, I learned about an innovate approach to community building sponsored by the United States Department of Housing and Urban Development.

The U.S. Department of Housing and Urban Development had begun offering Hope VI grants to help eligible communities replace outdated public housing with mixed- use developments. In cities across America, crime and drug infested public housing sites were torn down. Through Hope VI grants, cities began building mixed income developments that offered support services to eligible community residents. The program recognized that simply building new buildings does not in and of itself build community.

The definitions below of community and development provide more support and clarity of the community development process (Theodori, 2004, 2007).

- **Development in Community**: refers to physical construction of assets such as housing and community facilities
- **Development of Community**: refers to the strengthening of relationships and bonds among people
- **Community as Territory-free**: refers to the social groupings of individuals (i.e., African American community)
- **Community as Territory-based**: refers to a shared space or territory that provides a sense of identity and place

In addition, Theodori (2007) states that community development "is purposive, positive, and structure-oriented action and exists in the efforts, as well as achievements, of people willing to work together to address shared interest and solve common problems" (p.9). Simply put, community development is about working towards a shared vision for positive and strategic community change.

Needs-based versus Asset-based Community Development

Community development practitioners employ needs-based and asset-based strategies to foster strategic community change. Needs based strategies focus on what is going wrong in the community. Hence, needs-based community development strategies are concerned with overcoming gaps and deficiencies.

Typically, community development practitioners conduct a community needs assessment to ascertain the level and extent of need. The community needs assessment examines needs based on social, economic, and demographic trends. Therefore, need is often based on a gap between what is and what should be in the community.

On the other hand, asset-based community development strategies focus on what is going right in the community. Asset-based community development strategies seek to build on a community's strengths rather than on its weaknesses. In some communities, it can be a real challenge to identify such assets. John Kretzman and John McKnight (1993) are credited with advancing a process of identifying assets in communities for the purpose of community development. Kretzman and McKnight (1993) outline three principles of asset-based community development.

1. The process begins with the community, its residents, institutions, and associations.
2. The process is internally focused.

3. The process is relationship driven—building and rebuilding relationships among local institutions, residents, and associations.

I believe asset-based community development is more consistent with the values and worldview of churches and faith-based ministries. Asset-based development interjects faith into the process. The Biblical view of faith is "the confidence in what we hope for and assurance about what we do not see" (Hebrew 11:1, New International Version). In other words, asset-based development views a community the way it could be, rather than the way it is. Without a view of hope, it is easy to get discouraged and feel overwhelmed by the enormity and complexity of needs and challenges that exist in underserved communities.

Faith is a powerful ally when it is used in the context of community development. As a consultant, I have facilitated many focus groups with community residents from distressed communities. What I have learned is that people with little or no means have a deep faith in the possibilities of tomorrow. These individuals look past what is and focus on what could be. I have also observed that people who have the least often give the most and are more willing to make sacrifices. This is the paradox that Jesus taught the Disciples in Mark 12. The Bible states, "this poor widow has put in more than all those contributing to the treasury. For all of them have contributed out of their abundance, bus she gave out of her poverty" (Mark 12:43-44, New International Version).

In short, community and community development are dynamic and fluid concepts that carry multiple meanings. The boundaries of community may be loosely or narrowly defined. A religious community may have more narrowly defined boundaries than other communities based on its core values and beliefs. I believe community development is a people-and principle- centered process that recognizes both need and assets and then develops a strategy to solve problems in the community. This requires a collaborative framework, structure, and organizational capacity to implement strategies in concert with the community.

Guiding Principles of Christian and Faith-based Community Development

The following principles are not exhaustive and should be considered provisional.

Principle 1: Christian community development should be consistent with the moral teachings and philosophy of Jesus Christ. Moreover, it should be driven by core values such as love, redemption, and hope. Christian community development is a process of renewal; it seeks ways to promote wholeness.

Principle 2: Christian community development finds its purpose within the context of the Great Commission, which encourages Christians to spread the gospel and win new converts for Christ. This is accomplished by building and sustaining positive relationships with the community. The church has to win hearts before it can change minds and change communities.

Principle 3: Christian community development is focused on future possibilities and what could be. It is asset based as opposed to needs based. Faith is all about encouraging others that change can happen.

Principle 4: Christian community development initiatives should be transformative. That is, community development initiatives must advocate strategies that transform communities from the inside out and not the outside in. It must advocate strategies that have a long term and sustainable impact upon the community. To this end, transformative community development is not tactical, but strategic and future oriented.

Principle 5: Christian community development initiatives should be inclusive and express the character and wishes of the community. Too often, community development initiatives are about what funders and sponsors want rather than what the community wants.

Exercise 1. Understanding Community Development through Nehemiah

Working in teams of 4-6 or individually, read the book of Nehemiah (Holy Bible) Chapters 1-8 and answer the questions below. Allow time for discussion and reflection on the process.

1. How does Nehemiah practice community development? Is Nehemiah concerned with the development of community, community development or both?
2. What need does Nehemiah address in the community and why?
3. What assets does Nehemiah have at his disposal? How does Nehemiah organize and use these assets to advance his vision?
4. What opposition does Nehemiah face and how does he overcome it?
5. What are the outcomes of Nehemiah's work?
6. What is the significance of celebrating once the wall was completed?
7. How does Nehemiah measure success?

CHAPTER 3

Discovering Core Values

Examine yourselves to see whether you are in the faith; test yourselves. Do you not realize that Christ Jesus is in you—unless, of course, you fail the test?
2 Corinthians 13:5-6, NIV

When it comes to leading community-based change, churches and faith-based organizations should be intentional about their core values and beliefs. Milton Rokeach (1973) who is widely regarded as a pioneer of research on human values defines values as multifaceted standards that guide conduct in a variety of ways. Simply put, values communicate what is truly important to the church or ministry. I have observed that church leaders work long and hard on establishing and communicating their visions for the future. In the process, they fail to communicate their values, which help to underwrite their vision.

Values can be expressed through doctrine, statements of faith, annual budgets, or other ministry initiatives. These artifacts communicate what the church believes is important. Specter (2007) explains that there is tension between an organization's espoused values and enacted values. Espoused values are the values called upon by individuals to explain or justify their course of action. For example, the espoused values of hypothetical Community Church may be:

1. Acceptance: We believe in forgiveness.
2. Compassion: We believe in caring for the spiritual and material needs of others.
3. Relevance: We believe in being relevant to modern day followers of Christ.
4. Hope: We believe in preaching and teaching that inspires and gives hope, meaning, and purpose.

The enacted values, on the other hand, are the values that are implicit in that course of action or pattern of behavior (Spector, 2007). From the values of the hypothetical Community Church, it may be implied that the church enacts the values of human dignity. The values of human dignity affirm the life of people regardless of race, gender, color, or creed. This is important because society often assigns individual worth based on wealth, power, and status in the community.

The problem in organizations today is that leaders and followers are no longer speaking the common language of values (Hackman and Johnson, 2004). "This common language promotes unity, encourages loyalty, and enables individuals to make decisions on their own" (p. 158). The espoused and practiced values are the moral and ethical guideposts by which leaders and organizations defend their actions. Furthermore, Clawson (2003) adds:

> A major challenge for leadership is to be congruent with their stated values. Few things are more demoralizing…to see a gap between a leader's walk and his talk. When you reflect on, identify, and declare your…values, you had better be sure you are a good role model for them (p. 168).

Unfortunately, we see many examples in the course of our everyday lives of institutions and people behaving inconsistently with their espoused values. The news is filled with stories of trusted members of the community— police officers, teachers, and elected officials-committing shameless acts against the very people they swore to protect and serve. These inconsistencies undermine trust and create feelings of resentment and anger from the community.

How does the Bible Model Values for Community

The Apostle Paul's New Testament letters to Christian communities promote values that leaders and organizations should espouse and enact when engaging in community development activities. Aubrey Malphurs (2004) in his book, *Values-driven leadership*, argues that leaders must build an organization on the values that people already embrace, and not what you hope they will embrace in the future. Moreover, congregations should be viewed as caring communities. As caring communities, congregations try to emulate first-century followers of Christ who came to be known for the love and support of one another (Wuthnow, 2004).

In my experience, the values of unity, diversity, and love are fundamental to a people- centered process of building and developing community. In the paragraphs below, I provide a concise, but careful examination of some of the Apostle Paul's New Testament Letters and Epistles as a basis for understanding the influence of values.

Unity

The Apostle Paul's Letter to the church at Corinth suggests that the church should create a shared vision of unity when it comes to community development. Paul writes: "Now I appeal to you, brothers, and sisters, by the name of our Lord Jesus Christ, that all of you be in agreement and that there by no divisions among you, but that you be united in the same mind"(I Corinthians 1:10, New International Version).

The divisions that Paul addressed were concerning the proper exercise of charisma or gifts. For Paul, the diversity of gifts is for the profit of all members of the church as opposed to the individual. In Ephesians 4, Paul explains that diverse ministry gifts are for the edification and growth of the body of Christ, which is the church.

In addition, the Apostle Paul often encouraged followers to practice *koinonia* or fellowship and sharing among believers. Michalko (2006) explains that the spirit of *koinonia* is based on the principles of dialogue, collegiality, clarifying thinking, and honesty. Church and faith-based leaders must be willing to engage the community and work in partnership to accomplish strategic goals. According to Obama (1990):

> Equally important, it enables people to break their crippling isolation from each other, to reshape their mutual values and expectations and rediscover the possibilities of acting collaboratively — the prerequisites of any successful self-help initiative (pp. 35-40).

To create unity, Paul employed a strategy of using cultural symbols and familial language to connect with his followers. For example, Paul ends his letter to the Corinthians by instructing them to "Greet one another with a holy kiss" (I Corinthians 16:20, New International Version). Moreover, Paul encouraged Philemon to receive Onesimus, a runaway slave, as a brother. "Perhaps this is the reason he was separated from you for a while, so that you might have him back forever, no longer as a slave, but more than a slave, a beloved brother"(Philemon 1:15-16, New International Version). Culturally, Paul used other elements of Roman society, such as sporting and entertainment, to connect with followers. Paul in I Corinthians 9:25 states, "Athletes exercise self-control in all things; they do it to receive a perishable wreath, but we an imperishable one" (New International Version).

Diversity and Inclusion

One of the criticisms levied against the church is that the church is too insular and only looks out for its own. Non-members need not apply. However, people in need often turn to the church because they believe the church will provide services without preconditions. This is where the church is different from secular social services agencies. Secular social services organizations place preconditions on receiving assistance, such as families must fall below a certain income or have few if any assets.

However, income can be misleading when a family may have a lot of debt or a child that requires extensive medical care. These families fall into the category of being too poor to be rich and too rich to be poor. Harris and Sherblom (2008) explain that diversity does not make life easier. "It is often simpler when we share cultural values, common experience, and basic assumptions with those whom we interact" (p. 88).

Diversity requires that we are intentional about engaging others whose worldviews and life experience differ from our own. This is a lot easier said than done. I believe that ethnocentrism has no place in community development. To believe that one is culturally superior to another human being does not affirm their humanity.

It has often been said that Sunday morning at 11 a.m. is the most segregated hour in America. However, in Galatians 3:28 Paul wrote: "there is no longer Jew nor Greek, there is no longer slave or free, there is no longer male or female; for are of you are one in Christ Jesus" (New International Version). Paul's notion of equality and diversity in the church opposes social hierarchy that was prevalent in Roman society. Society in the provinces of the Roman Empire was highly stratified. Social categories such as noble, wealthy, poor, slave, were deeply embedded into the cultural fabric of Rome

(Brown, 1997). Paul articulated a model of community that conferred the values of human dignity upon individuals who were marginalized by society.

Love

The Apostle Paul's writings also suggest that the value of love should be at the center of any church or faith-based community development initiative. In I Corinthians 13, the Apostle Paul declared that love is the single most important motivational factor behind everything we do in our lives. "If I give away all my possessions, and if I hand over my body so that I may boast, but do not have love, I gain nothing" (I Corinthians 13:3).

In other words, if the church builds new housing for the poor or feeds the homeless, but does not have love, then their labor is in vain. Corey and Corey (2006) state that "our fear can lead us to seal off our need for love, and it can dull our capacity to care about others" (p. 195). Because leaders often want to appear strong, the display of love may be withheld for fear of appearing weak or overly sensitive. However, as Paul articulates in I Corinthians 13, love should be expressed through our actions such as being patient with followers and demonstrating acts of kindness.

In short, church- and faith-based organizations should establish core values to guide the community development process. More importantly, the church should behave consistently with these values to effectively built trust and social capital in the community. Leadership is values-based, which necessitates that leader lead with heart and character. If the church does not operate consistently with its core values, any vision or strategy, no matter how grand, will not be fully realized.

Use the core values audit on the following page as a guide to help you discover your core values. Note how many values correspond to the community. These values will be important later as you structure your community and strategic planning process.

Exercise 2. A Core Values Audit

Directions: (To be completed by the pastor or chief executive as a personal values audit.) Rate each of the values below, 1 to 5, 1 being the lowest and 5 being the highest.

____1. Volunteerism and Servant Leadership

____2. Equipped Lay Ministry

____3. Bible-centered Preaching and Teaching

____4. The Poor and Disenfranchised

____5. Creativity and Innovation

____6. Global Missions

____7. Acceptance and Love

____8. A Well Maintained Church Facility

____9. Financial Stewardship

___10. Change

___11. Hospitality and Fellowship

___12. Cultural Relevance

___13. Diversity

___14. Excellent and Well Managed Ministries

___15. Sense of Community

___16. Evangelism and Outreach

___17. Strong Families

___18. Grace and Forgiveness

___19. Music and Prophetic Arts

___20. Sacrificial Living

___21. Social Justice

___22. Committed Christians (discipleships)

___23. Charity (giving)

___24. Economic Justice

___25. Civil Rights

___26. Christian Education

___27. Traditionalism

___28. Equal Rights

___29. Other:

Write down all core values, but not more than 12, that received a rating of 4-5. Now rank these according to priority by placing the number 1 in front of the highest, 2 in front of the next highest, and so on. The top six are your core values.

(Framework adapted from Values-Driven Leadership by Aubrey Malphurs)

CHAPTER 4

Evaluating Organizational Ministry Capacity

Just as a body, though one, has many parts, but all its many parts form one body, so it is with Christ,
1 Corinthians 12:12, NIV

The primary criticism of seminary education is the lack of practical application of the coursework. I believe such advanced preparation in biblical exegesis is important for preaching and teaching, but the curriculum should be more focused on developing competencies in leadership and strategy. Ministry requires leadership, and leadership is ministry in my view because it is concerned with serving others.

Churches are struggling with how to integrate spiritual and organizational disciplines into a coherent practice of pastoral leadership. Seminary training and ordination requirements often do not adequately prepare leaders for the institutional realities of ministry (Mann, 2005). More and more, the value of a seminary education is being questioned and compared to other degree fields such as leadership that has more universal application.

The realities of poverty, opioid addiction, HIV and AIDS require skills in strategic planning, community organizing, financial resource development, and organizational design to deliver effective programs and services that have a lasting impact. Furthermore, effective strategy formation for community development cannot take place in a vacuum. Community development recognizes that coalitions and partnerships with diverse stakeholders are necessary to address community problems.

In addition, Higgins and Mcallaster (2004) suggest that effective strategy formation must be followed by subsequent changes in strategy execution factors: organizational structure and leadership capacity. McGrath (2002) points out that the business community is often highly critical of the church because of outdated management practices and structures that inhibit it from achieving its stated goals. For example, decisions in large bureaucratic church organizations follow a strict chain of command. The chain of command works to ensure proper procedures are followed. However, these same procedures are often too slow to respond to changes in the external environment. Thus, members of the organization lack the power and flexibility to respond to problems and events as they emerge.

In large bureaucratic organizations, flexibility and the discretion to respond to disruptions that veer outside of the parameters set by the organization may require substantial work (Montuori, 2003).

Bureaucracies are bound by red tape. This red tape restricts the flow of information. In these organizations, ideas flow upward, decisions flow downward, but members often lack the power to implement the decision. This can give rise to feelings of alienation, frustration, and resentment towards the organization.

Gareth Morgan (1993) in his book, *Imaginization,* suggests that we cannot hope to create new organizational forms in old ways of thinking. These old ways of thinking are so ingrained that they are difficult to move beyond. "People do not understand why things that have worked so well up to now no longer do the trick" (Handy, 1995, p. 55).

An early 20th century organizational theorist, Frederick Taylor, espoused the belief that management should do all the thinking while workers perform the task. Taylor's principles of scientific management included the division of labor into narrow specializations, centralized decision making, hierarchical organizational structures, and downward communication patterns. Morgan (1998) asserts that Taylor's approach effectively splits the worker by advocating the separation between thinking and doing. In the church, Taylor's notion of scientific management is often expressed when leaders suggest that members should only operate narrowly in the "one" gift that God has given them.

It is my belief that the church must move toward organizational structures that are flexible and adaptive. This would allow the ideas, gifts, and knowledge of its members to be expressed more freely.

Success and survival of post-industrial organizations depend on creativity, innovation, discovery, and inventiveness (Martins and Terblanche, 2003). Moreover, organizations need innovative processes and environments that encourage and reward creativity rather than stifling the creative spirit with systems and procedures that focus on control and command (Ashkenas et al., 2002). Nowhere is this more evident than in churches that thrive on freedom of the Holy Spirit, gifts, and talents of its members. Members need opportunities to serve in broad areas that interest them provided that it fits into the mission and vision of the church (Roffe, 1999).

Developing a Mission Statement

The church must also develop mission and vision statements that articulate its commitment to community development. "A mission statement is developed by the group to explain to external members or clients what the organization does and how it carries out its task" (Hoyle, p. 20). The mission statement of the church is often expressed through the Great Commission found in Matthew 28:19-20: "Go therefore and make disciples of all nations, baptizing them in the name of the Father and of the Son and of the Holy Spirit, and teaching them to obey everything that I have commanded you" (New International Version).

The church's mission statement answers the questions, what are we supposed to be doing? What marketplace do we serve? What end goal are we working towards? An example of a mission statement for Community Church might read:

The mission of the Community Church is to fulfill the Great Commission as found in Matthew 28. Our Mission is to go into the entire world and make disciples of all persons.

Clarifying the Vision

The vision statement on the other hand, provides inspiration and paints a picture of what the future will look like. Collins and Porras (1996) explain that a well-conceived vision consists of two major components: core ideology and envisioned future. According to the authors, core ideology is the glue that holds the organization together as it grows. Core ideology also speaks to the organization's core values, which are its guiding beliefs of the organization. The envisioned future involves the unrealized dreams, hopes, and aspirations of the organization (Collins and Porras, 1996). An example of a vision statement of Community Church is below:

> *Our vision at Community Church is to unite people from all walks of life and backgrounds under the transformational power of the love of Christ.*

The above vision communicates a future where people live in harmony. The vision statement also envisions a future where peoples' lives are changed and reflective of the saving power and grace of Jesus Christ.

The vision must go beyond lofty dreams and be put into action. The church cannot continue to blame the devil for its failure to act. I fully believe in James' declaration that faith without works is dead- no life, no power, and no change (James 2:17).

Leaders must bring the vision to life by rolling up their sleeves and participating with everyone else. Hence, church leaders should be prepared to make sacrifices and risk political and social capital to advance the vision. Henry Mintzberg, a leading scholar on strategy asserts that leaders mistakenly detach thinking and execution during the strategy formation process. The end result is strategies that are shortsighted, unlearned, disjointed, and do not capture the culture and nuances of organizational life (Mintzberg, 1994).

Perhaps no leader understood this better than Peter in the books of Acts. In Acts 2, God revealed His vision for the community after the outpouring of the Holy Spirit. The vision was first spoken to the Prophet Joel (Joel 2:28-32). To paraphrase, God said He would pour out His spirit on all flesh, and your sons and daughters shall prophesy, and young men shall see visions and old men shall dream dreams. However, Peter's vision did not stop here, but he continued to labor, preach, baptize, and exhort people until they were baptized and accepted Christ. According to the Bible, the fruit of Peter's efforts was three thousand souls (Acts 2:41).

All in all, the church should create an organizational structure based on core values of unity and equality to address community problems. Act 2:44-45 states: "All who believed were together and had all things in common; they would sell their possessions and goods and distribute the proceeds to all, as any had need" (New International Version). The Apostles recognized that the community is more than the sum of its parts.

Exercise 3. Developing a Mission and Vision Statement

Mission Statement:

What is the purpose of your organization?

Who do you serve and why?

What services does your organization provide?

Vision Statement:

What future do you envision for your organization?

How will the community be different as a result of the work you intend to do?

What positive change will you effect?

What dreams do you have for the future?

CHAPTER 5

Overview of Strategic Planning

It's better to be wise than strong; intelligence outranks muscle any day. Strategic planning is the key to warfare; to win, you need a lot of good counsel, Proverbs 24:5-6, MSG

When formulating a strategy, the church must understand its capacity and core competencies before it launches a community development initiative. For instance, a church that wants to build affordable housing should have or acquire expertise in construction, financing, or asset management. Even childcare facilities have complex requirements for how much square footage is needed per child and the safety of playground equipment. If the church purchases property for any community development initiative, it should review the zoning to ensure it is compatible with the future use of the property.

Exploring the Dynamics of Strategic Planning

Most strategic planning models have a few basic elements such as reviewing the vision and mission and developing clear goals, objectives, and action plans. Strategic planning is often distinguished from operational or short range planning because it is used to chart long-term direction. Strategic planning is about developing a shared vision for the organization's future, then determining the best way to achieve this vision (Berry, 1998). Lauenstern (1986) asserts that the purpose of strategic planning is to help executives evaluate longer terms implications of courses of action in hopes of making better decisions. Lauenstern explains that to be useful, strategic planning must provide insight on the following:

- o   A range of possible future developments and how to be prepared for them;
- o   Where to allocate resources for long-term returns;
- o   What capabilities must be developed for competitive success; and
- o   How to design and organize the organization so that various activities contribute to each other and provide for maximum results.

Strategic planning should be viewed as a tool that informs decision-making and produces a blue print for the future by looking objectively at where the organization is (Bryson, 1995). "Strategic planning should promote wise strategic thought and action on behalf of an organization and its stakeholders" (p. 9). Strategic planning can also help a church adapt to a changing environment, take advantage of opportunities created by change, and reach agreements on major ministry initiatives. Strategic planning offers other benefits such as improved collaboration and shared expertise to deal with complex issues surrounding the community (Miglore, Stevens, & Loudon, 1994).

Strategic Planning Tools

A popular strategic planning tool is a SWOT analysis or an appraisal of the organization's *Strengths, Weaknesses, Opportunities, and Threats*. A SWOT analysis provides a simple method to collect and organize information so that multiple factors can be considered in the decision-making process. Hill and Jones (2013) explain that the purpose of a SWOT analysis is to identify strategies to exploit external opportunities, counter threats, build on and protect organizational strengths and eradicate weaknesses. "More generally, the goal of a SWOT analysis is to create, affirm, or fine turn a company specific business model that will best align, fit, or match a company's resources and capabilities to the demands of the environment in which if operates (Hill and Jones, 2013, pg. 19).

Table 1 below is an example of a SWOT Matrix to clarify the process.

Table. 1. The SWOT Matrix

Conditions	Internal	External
Favorable	Strengths	Opportunities
Unfavorable	Weaknesses	Threats

An example of a SWOT analysis is below for a hypothetical Church.

Strengths

- We have strong and stable leadership; only 2 pastors since we were founded in 1960s
- We are family and community centered; the majority of our membership is related by blood or marriage and lives in close proximity to the church
- We recently renovated our Fellowship Hall and added a new technology wing with 20 computers
- We have a small ministry team; little hierarchy

Weaknesses

- We are a small congregation; too few people in key leadership positions
- Small operating budget
- Congregation is too inwardly focused; few outreach or missions programs

Opportunities

- The city is building a new school in our community scheduled to open next year
- There are new homes under construction and the community is attracting new residents

- We are one of five churches within a 3 miles radius of the community

Threats

- Aging congregation; youth leave the church after graduation and few return
- Influx of new and upper-class residents is driving up cost of housing making it unaffordable for people who have always lived here.

The SWOT analysis is easy to use and allows the strategic planning team to see the organization as a whole in relation to its environment. By conducting an internal (strengths and weaknesses) and external analysis (opportunities and threats), information that is vital for the church's survival and growth should be revealed. The SWOT analysis therefore, should scan present and future trends, resource needs, collaborations, and potential partnerships. Scanning should specifically focus on social, economic, and political trends surrounding the church. For example, socials trends, poverty and economic trends, per- capita income can be used to paint a portrait of the community and help leaders consider the causes and impacts of these trends.

When examining the environment, churches and faith-based organizations should examine six key areas: political, economic, social, technological, legal, and ecological contexts. In business strategy, this is referred to as a PESTLE analysis. Palmer et al (2017) assert that a PESTLE analysis as a method, helps organizations understand complex trends. Aubrey Malphurs in his book *Advanced Strategic Planning*, encourages churches to also examine the spiritual and philosophical environment which includes the worldviews and values of members and stakeholders involved. For example, much has been written about the decline in religious participation among the millennial generation. Churches should consider how this might impact their ability to attract and retain new members. I also suggest that ministries should examine the natural and built environmental context as well. This includes examining new and existing businesses in the community, transportation infrastructure, housing development, and changes in zoning laws that could impact the churches ability to engage in development activities. An example of each context, key indicators to look for, and questions to consider is found in Table 2.

Table 2. Sample PESTLE Analysis

Scanning Categories	Trends to Look For	Questions to Ask
Political	Changing Political Dynamics, rise in Popularism, Nationalism, Evangelicalism	What impact will the changing political climate have on ministry and the availability of resources?
Economic	Debt, Income Disparities, Unemployment Rate	How might an economic recession, rising poverty, and increasing rate of home foreclosures impact our outreach efforts in the community?

Scanning Categories	Trends to Look For	Questions to Ask
Social	Family and Marriage Patterns, Divorce Rates, Blended Families	How will the decline in traditional marriage affect our ministry?
Technological	Digital Technology, Social Media, Artificial Intelligence	What impact does technology have on the church and its ability to reach the community?
Legal	New Legislation, State and Federal Courts, Law Enforcement, Civil Rights, Church-State Issues	How will changes in local land-use policy, zoning, and transportation patterns impact our ability to grow and expand?
Ecological	Corporate Social Responsibility, Climate Change, Land Use Policies	What new forms of financing are available to support environmentally friendly community development projects?

Awareness of current trends can help churches prepare to meet their goals more effectively. The benefit of an environmental scan is that it can help the church assess whether or not certain community development initiatives are viable and actually needed. However, Cross (1987) cautions that most successful strategies do not arise logically from these data. Rather, they are informed gut feelings.

These data help to measure the reasonableness of the gut feelings once they surface.

The environmental scan should also include a list of churches or faith-based organizations providing similar services in the community. The last thing the church should do is duplicate services. Duplicating services creates competition and inefficiencies at the expense of the community.

In addition, strategic planning should include an appraisal of the church's internal environment or its strengths and weaknesses. While it is fairly easy to identify strengths, defining weaknesses can be painful. This is to say that organizations are sometimes unwilling to own their failures. Moreover, Byrson (1995) argues that organizations typically have plenty of quantifiable information such as salaries, supplies, and number of employees and volunteers. However, organizations have less of qualitative data or a command on information such as organizational culture, which impacts performance.

Table 3. Sample Internal Assessment

Internal Environment	Key Questions to Consider
Financial Viability	How will we raise money to sustain our community change initiatives?
Facilities	Do we have the facilities and infrastructure to facilitate ministry growth?
Generational Demographics	How many people do we have in each generational demographic? Which age groups are we experiencing growth or decline?

Internal Environment	Key Questions to Consider
Values	Is Community in our DNA?
Leadership Structure	How are decisions made? Is there a succession plan in place?
Gift and Talent Pool	Do we have the staff or the capacity to hire staff to engage in community change?

Strategic planning for community change should be highly participatory and involve key internal and external stakeholders, organizational leaders, and community groups to help define and shape the organization's future. Participation in strategic planning opens up the possibility of developing new understanding among various constituents about the work of the organization (Denhardt, 1985). Participation by diverse stakeholders in the process would help reduce inherent anxiety towards change and ensure that the end result is comprehensive and inclusive. Proverb 15:22 states: "without counsel, plans go wrong, but with many advisors they succeed" (New International Version).

Scenario Planning: A Supplemental Tool

The primary criticisms of strategic planning include its rationality, linear logic, and suggestion that the future is knowable. Hill and Jones (2013) posit that for strategic planning to work effectively, leaders must not only plan in their current competitive environment, but their future competitive environment as well. However, the notion that the future is knowable and can be predicted runs counter to the images of a God-controlled universe. The Bible states in Proverbs 19:21, "many are the plans in a man's heart, but it is the Lord's purpose that prevails" (New International Version). Moreover, Ogilvy (2005) argues that even if we could predict the future, we could not change it. In Matthew 6:34, Jesus states "do not worry about tomorrow, for tomorrow will worry about itself. Each day has enough trouble of its own" (New International Version).

Furthermore, we live in an age of uncertainty and rapid technological and environmental change, which is difficult to plan for. Increasingly, organizations need the ability to explore a wider range of possible and alternative futures. Scenario planning offers another tool in conjunction with strategic planning for churches and faith-based organizations as they prepare for the future. According to Schoemaker (1995):

> Scenario planning attempts to capture the richness and range of possibilities stimulating decision makers to consider changes they would otherwise ignore. At the same time, it organizes those possibilities into narratives that are easier to grasp and use than great volumes of data. Above all, however, scenarios are aimed at challenging the prevailing mind-set (p. 27)

Scenarios provide a framework for identifying what might happen rather than what will happen. A scenario is not a future reality, but a way of foreseeing the future and thereby shedding light on the present (Godet 2000). According to Godet, exploring the future is based on five questions:

1. What can and might happen?
2. What can I do?
3. What am I going to do?
4. How am I going to do it?
5. Who am I?

For Godet, the final question of who am I, underscores the importance of organizations knowing themselves. Simply put, organizations need to be true to who they are and recognize who they are not. The measure of a good scenario is plausibility, internally self-consistent, and useful to decision makers.

Developing Scenarios

Scenarios introduce imagination and creativity into the process and should challenge the conventional thinking inside the organization. Moreover, each scenario should contain interesting plots that capture the reader's attention and contain tensions that will ultimately be resolved. Peter Schwartz, co-founder of the Global Business Network, is considered by many to be a leading expert on scenario planning. In his book, *The Art of the Long View*, he outlined eight steps to scenario planning. Schwartz's eight steps are paraphrased and condensed into five to simplify the process.

Step 1. Identify Focal Issue or Decision. Begin with a specific decision or issue and then build out toward the environment. What will decision makers in your organization be thinking about in the near future? What are the decisions that have to be made that will have a long terms influence on the organization? For scenarios to be useful, they must teach lessons that are relevant. When determining focal issues, it is important to establish a time frame for the scenario. What will the future of the community look like in 2025?

Step 2. List the driving forces in the environment that are influencing change. What are the social, economic, political, environmental, and technological forces that are driving change? This step involves research to uncover the environmental drivers or shapers of change.

Step 3. Build narratives around each scenario. The scenario should have a beginning, middle, and end. Explain how you are going to get from A to B. How might you characterize each scenario? The goal is to end up with just a few scenarios to avoid a proliferation of different scenarios around every possible uncertainty.

Step 4. Examine the implications of each scenario by asking the 'what if' question. What are the opportunities and threats presented by each scenario? How probable or plausible is each scenario?

Step 5. Determine leading indicators or measurable trends you can monitor. How will you know if you are on target or moving towards the future?

Strategic planning is a means to an end and not an end in itself. Strategic planning is not a substitute for strategic thinking, acting, or leadership. Even the most well-crafted strategic plans are useless unless they can be implemented. Organizations should never assume that given a carefully developed strategic plan, results will follow.

Mintzberg et al. (1998) offers four fallacies of strategic planning: pre-determination, detachment, formalization, and strategic planning.

These fallacies are summarized below:

The fallacy of predetermination: To engage in strategic planning, an organization must be able to predict the course of its environment, to control it, or simply assume its stability.

The fallacy of detachment: Effective strategists are not people who abstract themselves from the daily details, but who immerse themselves.

The fallacy of formalization: This is the notion that systems can do better at tasks than flesh and blood.

The fallacy of strategic planning: The term strategic planning is an oxymoron. Because analysis is not synthesis, strategic planning has never been strategy making.

Lastly, Mintzberg (1987) argues that the word "planning" may be too rational and analytic. He suggests that the word planning should be replaced with crafting. Crafting a strategy suggests a more hands on approach that is developed through experience and commitment to the process. For the church, crafting a strategy is akin to the potter and the clay metaphor found in the Bible. The potter is the one who molds the clay, gives it shape, and form. The potter also determines the clay's function and end-use (Jeremiah 18; Isaiah 29:16).

Exercise 4. Using the SWOT Matrix below, try this exercise for your church

Strengths

positive internal

1.

2.

3.

4.

Weaknesses

challenging internal

1.

2.

3.

4.

Opportunities

positive external

1.

2.

3.

4.

Threats

challenging external

1.

2.

3.

4.

Based on your analysis, list three strategies that would build on your strengths and opportunities while countering weaknesses and addressing threats.

CHAPTER 6

Surveying the Land

My dear friends, don't believe everything you hear. Carefully weigh and examine what people tell you. Not everyone who talks about God comes from God. There are a lot of lying preachers loose in the world,
1 John 4:1, MSG

As we examined in the opening chapters, strategic initiatives should be based on clearly identified areas of need in the community. To do so, the church needs data and actionable intelligence on the community in question. Unfortunately, too many decisions are made on the basis of emotion and not on sound evidence and objective data.

The church should be prepared to use a variety sources and methods to get a better understanding of the issues and trends impacting the community. If data on a particular community are old or non-existent, the church may want to do a survey of the area. For small defined communities, a door-to-door survey may be appropriate, but for larger communities, a representative sample will work best. If the church is fortunate enough to be located near a university, it would be wise to approach the university for technical assistance. For state or publicly chartered universities, community service is a part of their mission.

If the church is not fortunate enough to be near a university, it could solicit the help of an outside consultant to design and administer a survey instrument or other data gathering techniques to assess the needs of the community. Before going down this road, I suggest that churches start with the U.S Census, which is taken every ten years by the federal government. The census provides a wealth of information on income, poverty, and homeownership status. This information is collected through surveys and samples of the general population.

The information collected by the census can be analyzed and reported by town, city, county, or zip code. In addition, local governments are also a good source for data on the community. Most cities and some small towns develop comprehensive plans and other planning documents that contain descriptive statistics on their populations as well. A trip to city hall or a few minutes on the city's website can save a lot of time when gathering data on your community. Moreover, these comprehensive plans can inform the church on future development opportunities under consideration.

Because these data from the census can become outdated, the church should be prepared to engage the community through focus groups, town hall style meetings, and in- depth interviews with keys leaders in the community to get a deeper insight into the lives of people. These and other qualitative techniques seek answers to questions by examining social settings and the individuals that inhabit these settings (Berg, 1998). Qualitative data are richer in the sense that they provide insight into the participants' values and worldviews that cannot be expressed numerically. Berg explains that "qualitative techniques allow researchers to share in the understanding and perception of others and to explore how people structure and give meaning to their daily lives (p. 7). When qualitative data are being used, the church will look for themes and patterns in these data that help articulate their meaning. The excerpt below summarizes data collected from a focus group session with a community in support of a strategic plan:

> Focus group participants articulated the need for progressive and collaborative leadership to solve problems confronting the community. These challenges included: economic development, education, environment, and the county's changing demographics. The community is becoming home to a growing senior, retirees, and Hispanic population. However, these groups are underserved when it comes to healthcare, education, and recreational opportunities. As one focus group participant stated: "diversity issues will be more important. We need in integrate the Hispanic community better. This has to be a part of what we do to create community. We need to focus on aging population. How do we deal with this as far as healthcare, retirement communities, and rest homes."

Furthermore, focus group participants expressed that the community will have to focus more intently on fostering an environment of inclusion and openness. The lack of diversity on boards, committees, and other decision-making bodies undermines trust. Diversity and inclusion strengthen the community because it offers new perspectives on challenging issues facing the community. The focus on diversity will need to include youth and seniors as well. Youth have few options after graduation and many leave and never return. When this happens, the community suffers and its social capital further diminishes. Seniors on the other hand, have time and expertise that could be utilized by schools, non-profits, and other civil groups.

Focus group participants also expressed that economic development should be balanced with environmental concerns and natural resources protection. The natural beauty of the community is one of its strongest assets. Economic development should be compatible with the green landscape. Increasing tourism may be an opportunity, but tourist need places to shop, eat, and play. Economic development should also include downtown redevelopment. Another focus group participant said "maybe if we had a movie theatre and more choices downtown," it would stop people from having to drive long distances to shop or enjoy a movie.

Improving education was also among the list of things the community must do to achieve any vision for the future. Low high school graduation rates have put the county at a competitive disadvantage when attracting jobs from other areas. Without a skilled and highly educated workforce, employers may continue to overlook the community when seeking places to grow and expand. While incentives may help attract employers in the short-term, it would do little to sustain economic development over the long haul.

By investing in education, youth will be able to compete in the global economy. This should also include investing in the local Community College through programs in math, science, and health services. The jobs of the future will require education in these core areas. The community cannot hope to rebuild the economy on textile and manufacturing jobs. Investing in education and technology will help encourage innovation and entrepreneurship, which has long been associated with the community.

In sum, to achieve any vision, it requires leadership. Without concerted leadership on multiple levels---government, business, non-profit, and the community, strategies to solve the community will continue to be fragmented and reactionary at best.

To assess the internal environment of the church, it would be useful to conduct an internal survey. The survey could ask questions related to the vision, mission, and values of the church. The survey can be mailed to members of the church, posted online, or completed on the church website. Online survey tools such as Survey Monkey and Google forms are easy to use and can provide analysis that is user friendly and easy to disseminate. Depending on the make-up of your congregation, you should decide which method to use before undertaking a survey. A mail survey will be more expensive because it has to be mailed out along with a stamped envelope for members to mail the survey back. If you have a large congregation, that can get very expensive. Another method may be to insert the survey in the Sunday bulletin and ask members to fill it out and place it in a drop box on their way out. I would do this for more than one Sunday to ensure everyone has a chance to respond.

At any rate, there is no substitute for good data. The church should be prepared to spend a fair amount of time accessing, collecting, and analyzing data. I recommend creating a team of socially conscious and capable people who can commit to the task of gathering and analyzing data for the strategic plan. The list below summarizes the other techniques that I have found useful for gathering data for the strategic planning process.

> *Scanning*-Scanning is based on a systematic survey of current newspapers, magazines, Web sites, and other media for indications of change (Cornish, 2004). When scanning, it is important to seek out diverse sources of information, competing views, and different perspectives.

> **Community Asset Mapping:** Similar to environmental scanning, community asset mapping attempts to uncover

existing assets or strengths in the community that can be used to leverage future development opportunities. This includes the social, intellectual, financial, and political capital present in the community (Ayers and Williams, 2013).

Brainstorming-The idea behind brainstorming is to bring a small group of people together to express ideas and defer judgment. Brainstorming helps to create an environment that will encourage the free flow of ideas, imagination, thought, and reflection on the problems facing the church or community (Michalko, 2006).

Trend monitoring-Trends viewed as important may be monitored, watched, and reported to key decision makers. Rising unemployment or increasing poverty in a community are trends that may signal the need for additional support and resources (Cornish, 2004).

Visioning-Visioning starts with a review of past events and the current situation. Then it moves on to envisioning desired futures and concludes with the identification of specific ways to move toward the desired future (Cornish, 2004).

More on Conducting Focus Groups

As mentioned, focus groups can be an effective means of gathering data and engaging the community. However, the structure and composition of focus groups can influence the strength and usability of the data collected. Sometimes that data collected from focus groups is only as good as the participants themselves. I have facilitated numerous focus groups and, invariably, there is always one participant who wants to dominate the discussion. I have also facilitated focus group sessions where it was laborious to get people to talk and open up. I have also noticed that small groups of 7-10 participants work better than larger groups.

With larger focus groups, it is harder to establish a rapport, put participants at ease, and keep people from discussing ancillary information that has nothing to do with the subject at hand. Nonetheless, focus groups can yield powerful group and individual experiences to shed light on a particular problem. Quite frankly, it is easy to collect secondary data on the community without talking to a single resident. For this reason, many organizations do not bother engaging the community in the first place. On the other hand, I have participated in community-based strategic planning processes where the community is tired of being asked the same one of two questions.

Below are a few principles for designing and facilitating focus groups.

1. ***Define the objectives of the research problem***. Develop a good understanding of the research problem and questions

that would shed light on the problem. Is the focus group the sole means of collecting data, or is it a part of several other research strategies?

2. ***Nature of the Focus Group.*** What are the group's characteristics? Does the focus group represent a broad cross-section of the community? Is it inclusive and representative of the community?

3. ***Atmosphere and Environment.*** The facilitator should go to great lengths to create a safe and welcoming atmosphere where participants can share freely. This includes keeping information discussed during the focus group confidential.

4. ***Active and Listening Facilitator.*** The focus group should be structured with an agenda and schedule start and stop times. However, the focus groups should not be so structured that spontaneous responses and ideas that were not a part of the original scope do not have an opportunity to be discussed or examined.

5. ***Preparation.*** The facilitator should be prepared well in advance of the focus group. The facilitator should provide guidance and structure for the participants, and give some indication of what the questions will be or the subject matter to be discussed. The lack of structure and preparation are sure ways to lose an audience and waste participants' time.

6. ***Research Assistance.*** There should be a division of labor. The facilitator cannot and should not attempt to facilitate,

observe the dynamics of the group, and record notes at the same time. The facilitator should be assisted by a research assistant that can take field notes, video or voice record, and help analyze and code these data.

7. *Analysis.* The data must be analyzed using methods that are reliable and valid. One method of analysis is to analyze the content of the statements made by the focus group participants. With this method, you are examining the frequency of words, looking for patterns and themes that emerge from these data.

For more information on research methods, see Berg, C. (1998). *Qualitative Research Methods for the Social Sciences*, Boston, MA: Allyn and Bacon.

CHAPTER 7

Strategic Planning Step by Step

Suppose one of you wants to build a tower. Will he not first sit down and estimate the cost to see if he has enough money to complete it? Luke 14:28, NIV

Strategic planning often means introducing organizational change. Change can be good or bad for the organization depending on the timing and scope of the change. Given this paradox, strategic planning can be a highly political and contentious process. Moreover, change can threaten individuals with a loss of status and power. For instance, I worked for a large bureaucratic organization that was not open to change or new ideas. I finally figured out that people are fearful of change because they had built their entire career on maintaining the status quo. Change meant learning new skills and embracing new ideas.

Managing change is also difficult because it means overcoming organizational rigidity. This can frustrate efforts to meet new environmental pressures. For example, the creation of a new ministry strategy may create internal conflict because resources have to be reallocated or shifted to implement it. According to Johnson-Cramer, Parise, and Cross (2007): "resistance is so difficult to diagnose and confront because it usually emanates from the two sources, an organization's culture and its informal structure (patterns of communication and interaction among members), which are most difficult to see" (p. 86). Resistance to change may also come from other sources such as core competencies and investment lock-in (De Wit and Meyer, 2005). For example, the better an organization is at something the more likely it is to favor those competencies that strengthen its competitive advantage. Investment lock-in happens when an organization commits a large sum of money and time to a specific activity and is therefore locked-in to it by nature of its investment.

As mentioned earlier, culture is perhaps the greatest source of resistance to change. Culture represents the dominant values, thinking, and behaviors of an organization and its members. "While strategy, structures, and specific people may change, culture remains rooted in the organization's past, sowing the seeds of conflict, and trauma" (Nadler and Tushman, 1997 p. 199). The culture of the church may be observed through its preaching, teaching, and worship styles. The culture may also be observed through the church's unique history and stories that have passed down to new members. Stories of survival, transition from one pastor to the next, or the construction of a new facility may provide insight into the culture of the church. Strategies that are inconsistent with the church's culture are less likely to gain the support of key members needed to implement the strategy. Tushman and O'Reilly (2002) provide further insight on organizational culture:

> Making changes in structure and systems is relatively easy; making changes in culture is not. Actively managing organizational cultures that can handle both incremental and discontinuous change is perhaps the most demanding aspect of the management of strategic innovation and change (p. 35).

To uncover potential conflicts and cultural barriers, an organization should conduct a values scan. A values scan is an examination of values of the members of the planning team, the organization, and the guiding philosophical principles the organization operates from (Goodstein, Nolan, and Pfeiffer, 1999). For churches and faith-based organizations, religious doctrine and theological beliefs may influence the strategies adopted. For example, if members of the church believe that church is about purity, holiness, and abstaining from worldly endeavors, it may resist notions that it should involve itself in the social issues such as drug addiction.

Gryskiewicz (1999) observes that there is a need for organizations to create cultures that recognize the need for an environment compatible with change and staffed with people who can adapt to changing opportunities. He argues that the organizations strive for equilibrium and consistency. By running an organization with no allowance for divergence, many organizations feel they can ensure continued success (Gryskiewicz, 1999). The world will not stand still while plans are being developed or implemented.

Strategic planning should be viewed as a dynamic and participatory process to create organizational and community change. Furthermore, community based strategic planning seeks to build a broad consensus among citizens, businesses, and organizations in the community to solve community problems (Berry, 2007). Strategic planning asks fundamental questions such as:

1) Where are we going?
2) How do we get there?
3) What is our blueprint for action?
4) How do we know if we are on track?

In addition, Berman (1998) suggests that community based strategic planning involves four phases.

1. The decision to initiate the process and the selection of key stakeholders and participants
2. Collecting data through the uses of SWOT or environmental scanning
3. Developing a mission, vision, values statement, identifying strategic issues, goals, strategies, objectives, performance measures, and timeline for implementation
4. Implementation of recommendations

Furthermore, Bryson (1995) offers a ten step Strategic Change Process, which provides structure to the strategic planning process. The following steps summarize Bryson's strategic change cycle:

Step 1: Initiate and agree on a strategic planning process. Identify internal and external stakeholders to be involved in the process. The goal is to facilitate a comprehensive and participatory process that has the support of the organization and its stakeholders. Ensure the process is inclusive of diversity-include young and old and women. The inclusion of women and youth are particularly important because neither group is adequately represented among the ranks of leadership. Form partnerships and alliances with outside groups whose values are similar and have a stake in the outcome.

Step 2: Identify Organizational Mandates. Review what the organization must do (its mandates). Review articles of incorporation, by-laws, and charters that outline the organization's formal mandates. Become familiar with the structure of the organization and understand how power and responsibility are distributed and who makes decisions.

Step 3: Clarify Organizational Mission and Values. The mission statement provides the justification and purpose for the organization's existence. Values, on the other hand, are the core beliefs of the organization — the nonnegotiable. The values communicate what the organization does and does not stand for. The values of an organization may be found in its budget. What does the organization spend money on? Values can also be clarified by using the storyboarding technique in Appendix C.

Step 4: Assess the organization's External and Internal Environment. This step involves looking at what is happening outside of the organization (external) and what is happening inside the organization (internal). This is often referred to as conducting a SWOT Analysis, or Strengths, Weaknesses, Opportunities, and Threats confronting the organization. The SWOT analysis is useful in identifying strategic issues the organization must address to improve and expand services in the community.

Step 5: Identify the Strategic Issues Facing the Organization. Strategic issues are fundamental questions or critical challenges that affect the organization's mandates, mission, values, and services. Strategic issues are those issues that the organization has the capacity to do something about. If the organization can't do anything about a specific issue, then the issue is not strategic. This is important because the church, like other organizations, does not have infinite resources. Said another way, can the church really be all things to all people? The church, as an organization, will be good at some things and terrible at others.

Step 6: Formulate Strategies and Plans to Manage the Issues. A strategy should communicate what an organization is, what it does, and why it does it. Effective strategy formation and implementation link strategic choices and actions with coherent and consistent patterns (culture) across levels and functions within the organization. Strategies should be consistent with the organizational culture. The new strategy may require changes in the organizational structure. New positions may have to be created with resources and authority to implement.

Step 7: Review and Adopt the Strategies and Plan. Once strategies have been formulated, the planning team should obtain official approval to adopt them and proceed with implementation. In order to secure the passage of any strategy, it is necessary to continue to pay close attention to the goals, concerns, and interests of all key internal and external stakeholders.

Step 8: Establish an Organizational Vision. The planning team should develop a description of what it should look like once it has successfully implemented the strategies and achieved its full potential. In other words, how will the organization or community be different as a result of the new strategy?

Step 9: Develop an Implementation Process. Creating a strategic plan is not enough. These strategies must be incorporated throughout the organization for them to become a reality. Successfully implemented strategies result in a new regime of implicit and explicit norms, behaviors, decision-making procedures, and structures.

Step 10: Reassess Strategies and Strategic Planning Process. The strategic planning process is a means to an end, and not an end in itself. Therefore, on-going monitoring and evaluation of strategies is needed to ensure the overall success of the new process.

The aforementioned steps in Bryson's strategic change cycle are not necessarily linear, but dynamic to fit the needs of the organization. "The process does not always begin at the beginning…a new mandate, a pressing issue, or failing strategy" (Bryson, p.38). Moreover, the process should be iterative as to allow the organization to repeat and refine steps to effectively address issues as they arise.

Bryson (1988) asserts that because strategic planning leads organizations to focus on what is important, it may also lead them to adopt big win strategies. However, big risks can also result in big losses. The financial services industry took big risks by giving mortgages to people who could not afford them. As a result, many banks have suffered colossal losses and some of the world's most recognizable banking institutions have gone out of business. Conversely, organizations can seek small wins by taking a more incremental and gradual approach. A small win strategy focuses on the essentials and is driven by the vision (Bryson, 1988).

In short, balancing the tensions between big and small win strategies is important for church and faith- based organizations. Faith leaders often feel compelled to tackle the most complex problems confronting society: poverty, world hunger, and disease. Furthermore, the Great Commission mandates that the church take the gospel into the world and make disciples. Strategic planning can help the church identify and implement the best strategies for improving the community and at the same time spread the good news of Jesus Christ.

CHAPTER 8

Leadership for Community Change

Whoever wants to become great among you must be your servant, and whoever wants to be first must be slave of all. For even the Son of Man did not come to be served, but to serve, and to give his life as a ransom for many."
Mark 10:43-45, NIV

Leadership is ability to influence others; second, the willingness to influence others, and third, the ability to do that in a way such that they respond willingly (Clawson, 2003). I believe that responding willingly is critical, as many community change strategies are forced upon the community by outside entities. The take it or leave it approach to community development has done little to build local leadership capacity.

Community change requires a diversity of leadership styles. There is no one size fits all. However, some models of leadership are better than others depending on the situation or nature of the task. When it comes to leadership in the church, charismatic leadership is frequently on display. There are those who believe that only people with extraordinary gifts should be in positions of leadership in the church.

Charisma is a Greek word that means gifts of grace or an endowment upon believers by the operation of the Holy Spirit. Max Weber (1947) described a charismatic person as one who exercised power through follower's identification with and belief in the leader's personality. According to Weber, charisma occurs when there is a social crisis, a leader emerges with a radical vision that offers a solution to the crisis, the leader attracts followers who believe in the vision, and the followers come to perceive the leader as extraordinary.

Followers who share a charismatic relationship with a leader are willing to transcend self-interest for the sake of the collective (i.e., community) and engage in self-sacrifice in the interest of the mission. Hence, followers consistently place an inordinate amount of confidence and trust in charismatic leaders (Howell and Shamir, 2005).

However, there is a dark or shadow side of charismatic leadership that followers should be aware of. For example, excessive optimism can also make it difficult for the leader to recognize flaws in their vision. When leaders "identify too closely with a vision, it undermines the capacity to evaluate objectively. The experience of early success and adulation of subordinates may cause the leader to believe that his or her judgment is infallible" (Yukl, 2002, p. 251).

In addition, communities would benefit from leaders who embrace servant leadership as a model. Servant leaders are not motivated by money, fame, recognition, or the like, but are motivated by the values of service. Servant leadership proposes that leaders should serve the needs of their followers. Robert Greenleaf (1977) is credited with coining the term servant leadership, but the concept has its foundation in Jesus' teachings as recorded in the Holy Bible. According to Greenleaf:

> The servant leader is a servant first...it begins with the natural feelings that one wants to serve, to serve first. Then conscious choice brings one to aspire to lead. The difference manifests itself in the care taken by the servant—first to make sure that other people's highest priority needs are being served.

Sendjaya and Sarros (2002) assert that servant leadership and charismatic leadership share common Biblical roots. "In fact, Weber developed his definition based on the word Charisma in the Bible where it is used as a basis or legitimacy for various functional roles and figureheads" (p. 57).

Communities also need leaders who are more transformational than transactional in their approach to community development. Transformational leadership occurs when one person engages with others in such a way that leaders and followers raise one another to higher levels of motivation and morality (Burns 1978). Transactional leadership involves an exchange process that may result in follower compliance with leader request, but is not likely to generate enthusiasm and commitment to task objectives (Bass 1985, Yukl, 2002).

Conversely, transformational leadership involves follower's feelings of trust, admiration, loyalty, and respect toward the leader. Transformational leadership increases follower motivation and performance more than transactional leadership, but effective leaders use a combination of transformational and transactional to accomplish objectives (Yukl, 2002).

Perspectives on Christian Leadership

For Christian leaders, the Bible is the moral code and standard by which leadership is practiced. The Bible offers many evaluations of good and bad leadership, right and wrong behavior. In the Book of Genesis, God instructs Cain on the proper way to offer a sacrifice. According to Genesis 4:7, God tells Cain: "If you do well, will you not be accepted?"(New International Version). Jesus, in his Sermon on the Mount, draws a parallel to the story of Cain and Abel. Jesus states: "if you remember that your brother or sister has something against you, leave your gift there before the altar and go; first be reconciled to your brother or sister, and then come and offer your gift" (Matthew 5:23-24, New International Version). The story of Cain and Abel, and Jesus' reinterpretation of it, should remind us that a leader's decisions and behaviors impact others. To this end, leadership is as much about the leader as it is their followers. In fact, leadership does not exist without followers.

Christian leadership is first focused on God and then on others. McKinney (2005) argues that true leadership is not selfish but involves considering the needs of others. In Matthew 6:33 Jesus says, "But strive first for the kingdom of God, and his righteousness, and all these things will be given to you as well" (New International

Version). Jesus' Sermon on the Mount challenges leaders to appeal to the higher authority (God) when giving guidance and direction to their followers. Moreover, the Sermon on the Mount encourages leaders to lead by example. Jesus admonishes leaders to "Beware of practicing your piety before others in order to be seen by them, for then you have no reward from your Father in heaven" (Matthew 6:1, New International Version).

Christian leaders should also exhibit positive characteristics such as passion and commitment, but in my opinion, none are more important than vision. The Bible states, "where there is no prophesy, the people cast of restraint" (Proverbs 29:18, New International Version). Miller (1995) argues that the contemporary church is hungry for visionary leaders who have an understanding of the way things really are. Sharing, and communicating the vision, provides followers with a road map and establishes unity in the body. According to Miller, "vision plus communication is the winning profile of leadership" (p. 67). Harris and Sherblom (2008) state:

> True leaders are expected to do more than simply conduct meeting, control agendas, and keep track of events. A key piece of leadership is the ability to hold onto an overall vision while moving a group through the process necessary to achieve that vision. Leaders need to set long-and short-term goals, focus attention on relevant activities (p. 261).

Furthermore, Christian leaders are also "other focused" and have an acute awareness of the needs and challenges of the people they lead and serve. Jesus admonishes his audience to examine their relationship with their neighbor in his discourse in the Sermon on the Mount. For example, Jesus says in Matthew 5:42: "if someone forces you to go one mile, go with him two miles. Give to the one who asks you, and do not turn away from the one who wants to borrow from you." Christian leaders inspire and motivate their followers to give and sacrifice on behalf of the organization.

All in all, community change requires a variety of leadership styles and models to increase opportunities for success. While social crisis may give rise to charismatic styles of leadership, it may not be sustainable overtime, particularly as the organization matures. Servant and transformational leaders can inspire followers to reach for something greater than themselves. Moreover, servant leadership is rooted in the philosophy of love and service. Jesus said, "no one has greater love than this, to lay down one's life for one's friends" (John 15:13, New International Version).

CHAPTER 9

Concluding Thoughts

The end of a matter is better than its beginning, and patience is better than pride, Ecclesiastes 7:8, NIV

Churches and faith-based organizations have a strategic opportunity to impact change in their communities. However, this opportunity may be lost unless a framework is developed that incorporates the dynamics of faith, strategy, and organizational development to solve complex problems. James 2:17 states: "so faith by itself, if it has no works, is dead" (New International Version).

The church must be the one institution that does not turn its back on people in need. Even as you read this book, jobs are being shipped overseas, banks are foreclosing on homes, and schools are failing to educate the nation's youth. I believe the church is the foundation of society and must lead by example. Martin Luther King Jr. said, "if the church does not recapture it prophetic zeal then it will become an irrelevant social club with no moral or religious authority."

Churches and faith-based organizations must also operate consistently with their core values. Values such as diversity and love can break down social barriers in communities and facilitate trust and cooperation. Community change is about wielding power and influence to benefit the common good rather than the narrow interest of a few. Strategic planning is a model that encourages change, active participation, and learning to increase church and organizational effectiveness.

References

Ayers, D.L., Williams, R. W. (2013). *To serve this present age: Social justice ministries in the black church*. King of Prussia, PA: Judson Press.

Ashkenas, R., Urlich, D., Jick, T., & Kerr, S. (2002). *The boundaryless organization: Breaking the chains of organizational structure*. San Francisco, CA: Jossey-Bass.

Berry, B. (1998). A beginners guide to strategic planning. *The Futurist*.

Berry, F.S. (2007). Strategic planning as a tool for managing organizational change. International Journal of Public Administration, 30,333-346.

Berman, E. (1998). *Productivity in public and non profit organizations: Strategies and techniques*. Thousand Oaks, CA: Sage Publications.

Berg, B.L. (1998). *Qualitative research methods for social science*. Boston: Allyn and Bacon.

Bobbe, R., Mendelson, J., & Schulmon, Y. (2000). The strategic planning trap: How to avoid it. *The Journal of Jewish Community Service*, Spring.

Brown, R. (1997). *An introduction to the new testament*, New York: Doubleday.

Bryson, J., & Roering, W. (1987). Applying private-sector strategic planning in the public sector. Journal of American Planners Association, winter, 9-21.

Bryson, J. (1988). Strategic planning: big wins and small wins. *Public Money & Management*.

Bryson, J. (1995). *Strategic planning for public and nonprofit organizations*. San Francisco, CA: Jossey Bass Publishers.

Chaskin, R., Joseph, M., & Chipenda-Dansokho. (1997). Implementing comprehensive community development: Possibilities and Limitations. *Social Work*, 42, 5

Chaves, M. (2001). Six myths about faith-based initiatives: Going by faith. *Christian Century*.

Churchill, M.C (2002). In bad faith? Possibilities and perils in the age of faith-based initiatives. Journal of the American Academy of Religion, 70 4.

Clawson, J.G. (2003). *Level three leadership: Getting below the surface*. Upper Saddle River, NJ: Prentice Hall.

Collins, J.C., & Porras, J.I. (1996). Development of your company's vision. Harvard Business Review, September-October.

Copeland, L.E. (1976). Church growth in acts. Missiology, 4 (1), 13-26.

Corey, G., & Corey, M.S. (2006). *I never knew I had a choice: Explorations in personal growth*. California: Thomson.

Cornish, E. (2004). *Futuring: The exploration of the future*. Bethesda, MD: World Future Society.

Creswell, J.W. (2003). *Research design: Qualitative, Quantitative, and mixed methods approaches*. Thousand Oaks, CA: Sage Publications.

Cross, H.R. (1987). Strategic planning: What it can and can't do. *SAM Advanced Management Journal*, 52,1.

Denhardt, R. (1985). Strategic planning in state and Local government. State and Local Government Review. Winter, 174-179.

De Wit, B., & Meyer, R. (2005). *Strategy synthesis: Resolving strategy paradoxes to creative competitive advantage*. United States: Thompson Learning.

Gardner, J. (1990). On leadership. New York: The Free Press.

Gibelman, M., & Gelman, S.R. (2002). Should we have faith in faith-based social services: Rhetoric versus realistic expectations. Nonprofit Management and Leadership. 13,1.

Goodstein, L., Nolan, T., & Pfeiffer, J.W. (1999). *Applied strategic planning: How to develop a plan that really works*. New York: McGraw Hill.

Godet, M. (2000). The art of scenario and strategic planning: Tools and Pitfalls. *Technological Forecasting and Social Change*, 65, 3-22.

Greenleaf, R.K. (1977). *Servant leadership: A journey into the nature of legitimate power and greatness.* New Jersey: Paulist Press.

Gryskiewicz, S. (1999). *Positive turbulence: Developing climates for creativity and innovation.* San Francisco: Jossey-Bass Publishers.

Hackman, M.Z., & Johnson, C.E. (2004). L*eadership: communication perspective.* Long Grove, IL: Waveland Press, Inc.

Handy, C. (1995). *The age of paradox.* Massachusetts: Harvard Business School Press.

Harris, E. T., & Sherblom, J. C. (2008). *Small group and team communication.* New York: Pearson.

Higgins, J.M., & Mcallester, C. (2004). If you want strategic change, don't forget to change your cultural artifacts. Journal of Change Management, 4, 63-73.

Hill, C., Jones, M. (2013). Strategic management: an integrated approach. United States, South Western

Howell, J.M., & Shamir, B. (2005). The role of followers in the charismatic leadership process: Relationships and their consequences. Academy of Management Review, 30,96-112.

Hoyle, J.R. (1995). *Leadership and futuring: Making visions happen.* Thousand Oaks, CA: Corwin Press, Inc.

Johnson-Cramer, M., Parise, S., & Cross, R.L (2007). Managing change through networks and values. California Management Review, 49, 3.

Kouzes, J., & Posner, B. (2007). *The leadership challenge.* San Francisco: John Wiley & Son, Inc.

Kretzmann, J.P, & McKnight, J. (1993). *Building communities from the inside out: A path towards finding and mobilizing a community's assets.* Evanston, IL: Institute for Policy Research.

Kretzmann, J.P.(2000). Congregations and communities. In Edward L

Queen II (Ed.), *Serving those in need (p.45-62).* San Francisco: Jossey-Bass Publishers.

Lauenstern, M. (1986). The failure of strategic planning. *The Journal of Business Strategy*, 6, 4.

Malphurs, A. (2004). *Values-driven leadership: discovering and developing your core values for ministry.* Grand Rapids, Michigan: Baker Books.

Malphurs, A. (2004). *Advanced strategic planning: A new model for church and ministry leaders.* Grand Rapids, Michigan: Baker Books.

Mann, A. (2005). Strategic planning as spiritual practice. *Clergy Journal*, 4-8.

Martins, E.C., & Terblanche, F. (2003). Development organizational culture that stimulates creativity and innovation. *European Journal of Innovation Management*, 6, 1.

McCarthy A., & Garavan T. (1999). Developing self-awareness in the managerial career development process: the value of 360-degree feedback and the MBTI, Journal of European Training, 23,437-445.

McGrath, A. E. (2002). *The future of Christianity*. Malden, Massachusetts: Blackwell Publishers.

McKinney, M. (2005). *The focus of leadership: choosing service over self-interest*. Retrieved from www.leadershipnow.com.

Michalko, M. (2006). *Tinkertoys: A handbook of creative thinking techniques*. Berkeley: Ten Speed Press.

Miglore, R.H., Stevens, R.E., & Loudon, D.L. (1994). *Church and ministry strategic planning: From concept to success*. Binghamton, NY: The Haworth Press Inc.

Miglore, R.H. (1998). *Strategic planning for ministry and church growth*. Tulsa, OK: Harrison House.

Miller, C. (1995). *The empowered leader: 10 Keys to servant leadership*. Nashville, TN: Broadman & Holman Publishers.

Mintnzberg, H. (1978). Patterns in strategy formation. Management Science, 24, 9.

Mintzberg, H. (1987). Crafting strategy, In *Understanding Nonprofit Organizations: Governance, Leadership, and Management*. Boulder, CO: Westview Press.

Mintzberg, H. (1987). The strategy concept I: Five Ps for strategy. *California Management*, 30, 1.

Mintzberg, H. (1994). The rise and fall of strategic planning. Harvard Business Review.

Mintzberg, H, Ahlstrand, B, Lampel (1998). Strategy safari. New York, NY: The Free Press.

Montuori, A. (2003). From strategic planning to strategic design: Reconceptualizing the future of strategy in organizations. *World Futures*, 59, 3-20.

Morgan, G. (1993). *Imagination: the art of creative management*. Loudon: Sage Publications.

Morgan, G. (1998). *Images of organizations, the executive edition*. San Francisco: Berrett-Koehler Publishers, Inc.

Nadler, D.A., & Tushman, M.L. (1997). *Competing by design: the power of organizational architecture*. New York: Oxford University Press.

Nygren, D. (1994). Outstanding leadership in non-profit organizations: Leadership Competencies in Roman Catholic Religious Orders. Nonprofit Management and Leaderships 4, 4.

Obama, B. (1990). Why organize? Problems and promise in the inner city. In *After Alinsky: Community Organizing in Illinois*. Springfield: University of Illinois at Springfield.

Ogilvy, J. (2005). Abstract: Scenario planning, art or science. *World Futures*, 61, 331-346

OpenSource Leadership Strategies Inc (2004 July). *Funding and Faith: Research about faith based organizations and initiatives* (Z. Smith Reynolds Foundation). Retrieved from http://www.zsr.org.

Palmer, I, Dunford, R., and Buchanan, D. (2017). Managing organizational change: A multiple perspective approach, New York, NY: McGraw Hill.

Rokeach, M. (1973). *The nature of human values*. New York, NY: The Free Press.

Roffe, I. (1999). Innovation and creativity in organizations: A review of the implications training and development. *Journal of European Industrial Training*, 23, 5.

Salamon, L. M. (1999). *America's nonprofit sector: A primer*. New York: The Foundation Center.

Sanders, I.T. (1998). *Strategic thinking and the new science*. New York: The Free Press.

Schoemaker, P.H.J. (1995). Scenario planning: A tool for strategic thinking. *Sloan Management Review*.

Schwartz, P. (1996). *The art of the long view: Planning for the future in an uncertain world.* New York: Doubleday.

Sendjaya, S., & Sarros J. C. (2002). Servant leadership: Its origin, development, and application in organizations. Journal of Leadership & Organizational Studies, 9, 57-65.

Spector, B. (2007). *Implementing organizational change: Theory and practice.* Upper Saddle River, NJ: Pearson.

Tamas, A., Whitehorse, Y., & Almante, O. (2000). Systems theory in community development. Retrieved from http://wwww.tamas.com/samples/source-do Systems_Theory_in_CD.pdf.

Tanner, M. (2001). Corrupting charity: Why government should not fund faith-based charities. *Cato Institute Briefing Paper*, 62.

Theodori, G.L. (2005). Community and community development in resource based areas: Operational definitions rooted in an interactional perspective. *Society and Natural Resources*, 18.

Theodori, G.L. (2007). Preparing for the future: A guide to community based planning. *The Southern Rural Development Center.* Retrieved from http://www.srdc.msstate.edu/publications/theodori_final.pdf.

Trites, A.A. (1988). Church growth in the book of acts. Bibliotheca sacra.

Tushman, M.L., & O'Reilly, C. (2002). *Winning through innovation: A practical guide to leading organizational change and renewal.* Boston, MA: Harvard Business School Press.

Vago, S. (2004). *Social change.* Upper Saddle River, NJ: Pearson.

Vital, A.C., & Keating, D.W (2004). Community development: Current issues and emerging Challenges. *Journal of Urban Affairs,* 26, 2.

Weber, M. (1947). *Max Weber: The theory of social and economic organizations.* (A. M. Henderson & Talcott Parsons). New York: The Free Press.

Wilson, I., & Ralston, B. (2006). *The scenario planning handbook: Developing strategies in uncertain times.* United States: Thomson-South-Western

Winston, B. (2002). *Be a Leader for God's sake.* Virginia Beach, VA: School of Leadership Studies Regent University.

Wuthnow, R. (2004). *Saving America: Faith-based services and the future of civil society.* Princeton, NJ: Princeton University Press.

Yukl, G., (2002). *Leadership in Organizations (5th ed).* New Jersey: Prentice Hall.

Zietlow, J. (2000). *Developing financial accountability and controls.* In Edward L Queen II (Ed.), Serving those in need (p.45-62). San Francisco: Jossey-Bass Publisher.

About the Author

Dr. Jimmy Arthur Atkins is the Founder and Senior Pastor of True Worship Christian Fellowship located in Cary, NC. As a bi-vocational pastor, Atkins serves as an Associate Professor at Pfeiffer University where he teaches courses on leadership, change, and strategy. While at Pfeiffer, Atkins has taken teams of students on global immersion programs to Germany, France, and China. Atkins has also taught and lived in Germany as a Visiting Professor at the University of Applied Sciences in Fulda, Germany.

He is a proud graduate of North Carolina A&T State University, the University of Delaware, and Regent University where he completed his Doctorate in Strategic Leadership. He has also completed graduate coursework in theological studies at Wesley Theological Seminary in Washington DC. Dr. Atkins is married to his wife Kecia and together they have two children, James Everett and George Walter.

APPENDIX A

Sample Strategic Planning Exercises

Exercise A1. Developing a Shared Vision

Directions

Divide participants into groups of 8-10 persons. Give each group member a stack of index cards, markers, and flip chart. Ask the group, "If you could rent the Goodyear blimp and fly it over your community in the year 2015, what three accomplishments would you flash on the side of the blimp for all to see? After these personal visions are written down by each individual, ask them to turn to the person at the table located on their right or left and share their vision of their accomplishments.

After both individuals have exchanged their visions, the group facilitator will ask each pair to share their partner's accomplishments with the entire group. Ask the person that had the most recent birthday to be the recorder of each accomplishment on a flip chart for all to see. The facilitator will then ask the group to look for patterns in the accomplishments in 2020 and seek the group's ideas on what each individual can do to assist the member to accomplish their visions. Several themes will emerge from the desired accomplishment, and the genesis of a collective vision will become obvious. After the group vision takes some shape, rewrite it on the flip chart.

After all groups present, take a refreshment break, ask the group to appoint a spokesperson to stand and tell the entire group workshop crowd the collective group vision and any individual visions that may diverge from the group vision. Someone should be designated to collect all the groups' flipcharts and prepare a collective set of visions for 2015. These visions can be a driving force in developing a shared vision for change in the community.

Source: Adapted from Hoyle, J.R. (1995). Leadership and futuring: Making visions happen, Thousand Oaks, CA: Corwin Press, Inc.

Exercise A2. Discovering Core Values Storyboarding

Begin the storyboarding session by explaining the four rules of the process. The rules should be written on the flip cards in the right and left corner of the room. The four rules are:

1. Suspend all judgment
2. Quantity, not quality
3. Please, no speeches
4. No killer phrases

Example of killer phrases include, we have never done it that way before or that's not in the budget. Explain the purpose of the storyboarding such as "to discover our core values." The first part of the exercise is a brainstorming, or creative thinking exercise. If the group is discovering the church's core values, for example, the participants call out what they believe the church's core values are. The recorders write the responses on the cards, and on person pins them to the board. This may go on for fifteen or twenty minutes. When the facilitator senses that the group has exhausted its ideas, then it is time to shift to part two. This is the workout phase of the process. During this time, the group will prioritize ideas, look for trends and reoccurring themes, and remove any duplicates or false concepts. The group should eliminate values that are not true of the ministry, toss duplicate values, and identify items that are not actually values. It may be helpful in prioritizing ideas to give each participant a limited number of color-coded labels. Then ask them to come up during the break and stick the label on the cards with the most important ideas. The participants would place the labels on the cards they believe are the actual values of the organization. Then you will be able to quickly eliminate values without any labels. When you are finished, collect all the cards and give them to a secretary who will compile them for future use.

Source: Adapted from Malphurs, A. (2004). Advanced Strategic Planning: A new model for church and ministry leaders. Grand Rapids, MI: Baker Books.

APPENDIX B

Strategic Planning Handouts

Mission Statement

Mission Statement:

What is the purpose of your organization?

Who do you serve and why?

What services does your organization provide?

Write out a well-crafted mission statement that would help people outside of the organization understand who you are.

Core Values

List 5-7 values that you believe best describes your church or ministry:

Visioning

In the space below, answer the following question. After you have answered, share your vision with the person on your right or left.

"If you could rent the Goodyear blimp and fly it over your community in the year 20__, what three accomplishments would you flash on the side of the blimp for all to see?

Environmental Scan/SWOT Analysis

In the spaces below, list 2-3 environmental trends impacting your organization.

1. Social

2. Technological

3. Economic

4. Environmental

5. Political

6. Legal

SWOT ANALYSIS

Strengths

internal factors

1.

2.

3.

Weaknesses

internal factors

1.

2.

3.

Opportunities

external factors

1.

2.

3.

Threats

external factors

1.

2.

3.

Goals, Objectives, Action Steps

Stated Goal:	
Objective:	
Steps to Accomplish Objective	
A.	
B.	
C.	
D.	

Action Steps	Person Responsible	Start Date	Date Completed

Sample Strategic Plan Outline

I. Introduction

    A. Need for Strategic Plan

    B. How the Plan was Developed

II. The Environmental Scan

    A. External Environment

        a. National Trends

        b. State and Local Trends

        c. Summary of Opportunities and Threats

    B. Internal Environment

        a. Organizational Activities

        b. Leadership and Management

        c. Organizational Structure

        d. Summary of Strengths and Weaknesses

III. Organizational Design

    a. Organizational Values

    b. Community Vision

    c. Organizational Mission

    d. Organizational Structure

IV. Objectives, Goals, and Strategies

    a. Organization in 3-5 Years

      b. Strategic Priorities

      c. Action Plan

V.   Monitoring and Evaluation

      a. Plan for monitoring strategies

      b. Plan for evaluating success

      c. Plan for updating the plan

APPENDIX C

Grant Writing

Grant Writing Basics

Churches and faith-based organizations may want to pursue external funding for community change initiatives through grants from governmental or private organizations. Some regard grants as free money, but they are sorely mistaken as grants have restrictions and may require organizations to comply with certain rules that may contradict the doctrine and philosophy of the church. For this reason, it is important for churches and faith-based organizations to consider setting up a separate entity that can manage grant related activities. Moreover, some grants and funders require churches to have 501 3 C status. Generally speaking, churches are presumed to be tax exempt, but 501 3 C is a separate IRS designation all together. Unless the church has achieved this status, it may not be eligible to apply for certain grants. Even then, one should consider organizational capacity and the time commitment required to successfully manage grant awards.

Nonetheless, there is no magic formula for winning a grant. I have seen poorly written grant applications and proposals get funded. Conversely, I have seen well written and detailed grants with the best intentions get rejected. The reasons why grants are funded or not funded vary widely. The decision to fund or not fund a grant depends largely on the priorities of the grant making organization. For example, some government and private foundations place emphasis on projects that create jobs, work to alleviate poverty, and expand educational opportunities. Grant applications that fall within these parameters will be more competitive than grants that have nothing to do with these issues.

I have found some general rules and guidelines that organizations should follow when seeking grants from public and private sources. The following 7 principles are not exhaustive but are intended to provide guidance for novices and less experienced organizations on grant writing and proposal development.

1. Know Your Audience: Grant seekers should do as much homework on the funding organization as possible before submitting a grant application or proposal. You should know and understand what types of projects the organization has funded in the past and will likely fund in the future. This information can be obtained from the organization's website, annual report, or by contacting the organization's development staff directly. This will help you avoid submitting an application to a funder that has no history or interest in your project.

2. Understand the Rules of Engagement. This principle is an extension of the first—understand the funding criteria and

how the grant funds will be dispersed if awarded. For example, some grant-making organizations may only fund organizations that are located within a certain geographic area, have been in operation for a certain number of years, and have a minimum operating budget. If your organization does not meet the criteria, then do not waste your time preparing an application or proposal that is most likely to get rejected. Furthermore, some grant making organization disperse funds on a reimbursement basis, which means that you will have to spend and commit funds to the project first and then submit receipts for reimbursement. If you are a small organization with a limited operating budget, you may not be in a position to spend money and then wait to be reimbursed.

3. Gather Appropriate Data and Sources. Grant writing is a research and data intensive process. This means spending time researching and gathering data to support your proposal. The people reviewing your grant application may be subject matter experts and practitioners in the field. They will have a firm understanding of the needs that exist and the research to validate this need. You should consult the latest and best available research on the problem or need your grant will solve. Without a well-defined and supported statement of need, your application does not stand a chance of being funded.

4. Focus on the Target Population. The grant application and proposal should be focused on the target population and

community being served. The grant is not about the organization in and of itself. The mistake organization make is that they spend too much time talking about themselves rather than the target population or the needs of the community. Do not waste valuable space in the application focusing too much on your organization. There are creative ways to weave information about your organization into the grant application while at the same time addressing the needs of the community.

5. Review the Evaluation Criteria. The evaluation criteria will outline how your application or proposal will be scored. It will outline the number of points each section of the application is worth. This should give you some indication as to how much time you should spend on each section. For example, if the budget accounts for one third of the total number of points, you should spend a fair amount of time detailing and supporting your budget. The evaluation criteria can be used as a guide to write from the perspective of the funding organization. In a sense, it communicates what the grant making organization is looking for in an application or proposal.

6. Write Clearly, Persuasively, and Concisely. The grant application or proposal is a professional document. It communicates something about you and the organization. Hence, it should be well written, organized, and free of spelling, grammar, and punctuation mistakes. The document should also be free of jargon, slang, or other language that does not

clearly communicate the purpose and scope of the project. The grant application should be convincing and persuade the reader to take action.

7. Be Visionary and Strategic. When writing a grant, it is important not to paint such a negative picture of the problem that the reader will lose hope that anything can or will make a difference. The application or proposal should be truthful, but optimistic and provide a transformational approach to solving the problem. The approach to solving the problem should be strategic, measurable, and builds on the strengths and core values of the organization.

Made in the USA
Coppell, TX
09 February 2021